AUTHOR

Daniele Notaro, born on 22 January 2002 in Lavagna, is a History student at the University of Genoa. Since his early teens he has cultivated a passion for the Second World War, focusing in particular on the events of the Regio Esercito in the 1930s and 1940s. Other topics of interest to him are the cobelligerent armed forces, the events of the Autonomous Units of the Italian Resistance and the Italian coastal defence from the 1930s to the end of the Second World War. He started to publish his first writings on the Tank Encyclopedia site in 2022 and was a contributor to the journal Military History in his last period.

PUBLISHING'S NOTES

None of unpublished images or text of our book may be reproduced in any format without the expressed written permission of Luca Cristini Editore (already Soldiershop.com) when not indicate as marked with license creative commons 3.0 or 4.0. Luca Cristini Editore has made every reasonable effort to locate, contact and acknowledge rights holders and to correctly apply terms and conditions to Content.
Every effort has been made to trace the copyright of all the photographs. If there are unintentional omissions, please contact the publisher in writing at: info@soldiershop.com, who will correct all subsequent editions.
Our trademark: Luca Cristini Editore©, and the names of our series & brand: Soldiershop, Witness to war, Museum book, Bookmoon, Soldiers&Weapons, Battlefield, War in colour, Historical Biographies, Darwin's view, Fabula, Altrastoria, Italia Storica Ebook, Witness To History, Soldiers, Weapons & Uniforms, Storia etc. are herein © by Luca Cristini Editore.

LICENSES COMMONS

This book may utilize part of material marked with license creative commons 3.0 or 4.0 (CC BY 4.0), (CC BY-ND 4.0), (CC BY-SA 4.0) or (CC0 1.0). We give appropriate attribution credit and indicate if change were made in the acknowledgments field. Our WTW books series utilize only fonts licensed under the SIL Open Font License or other free use license.

For a complete list of Soldiershop titles please contact Luca Cristini Editore on our website: www.soldiershop.com or www.cristinieditore.com. E-mail: info@soldiershop.com

Title: **ALBANIA'S ITALIAN OCCUPATION - THE ITALIAN ANSCHLUSS** Code.: WTW-056 EN
By Daniele Notaro
ISBN code: 9791255890805. First edition: March 2024.
Language: English; size: 177,8x254mm Cover & Art Design: Luca S. Cristini

WITNESS TO WAR (SOLDIERSHOP) is a trademark of Luca Cristini Editore, via Orio, 33D - 24050 Zanica (BG) ITALY.

WITNESS TO WAR

ALBANIA'S ITALIAN OCCUPATION
THE ITALIAN ANSCHLUSS

PHOTOS & IMAGES FROM WORLD WARTIME ARCHIVES

DANIELE NOTARO

BOOKS TO COLLECT

CONTENTS

INTRODUCTION..Pag. 5

THE END OF WORLD WAR I AND THE WAR OF VALONA..................Pag. 7

RELATIONS BETWEEN THE KINGDOM OF ITALY AND ALBANIA BETWEEN 1920 AND 1939..Pag. 11

THE ITALIAN INVASION PLAN..Pag. 17

THE ALBANIAN ARMED FORCES AND THE DEFENCE PLAN..................Pag. 25

    The landing and occupation of Albania......................................Pag. 34

    The actions of the Regia Aeronautica...Pag. 37

    The arrival of the other scales and new divisions......................Pag. 50

THE LOSSES..Pag. 71

CONSIDERATIONS ON ITALIAN OPERATIONS....................................Pag. 71

THE UNION OF ALBANIA WITH THE KINGDOM OF ITALY AND THE INCLUSION OF THE ALBANIAN ARMED FORCES IN THOSE OF ITALY....Pag. 73

    The Albanian Fascist Party and the Albanian Fascist Militia.......Pag. 73

    Albanian units of the Royal Army...Pag. 73

    Gendarmerie and Royal Carabiniers...Pag. 75

    Border Guard and Royal Guard..Pag. 75

    Albanian Royal Guard..Pag. 76

ALBANIAN RESISTANCE UNTIL THE ARMISTICE.................................Pag. 81

Appendix: Italian decorators during operations in Albania................Pag. 93

Bibliography...Pag. 97

Sitography..Pag. 98

INTRODUCTION

The Italian occupation of Albania, which took place in April 1939, is a subject that is scarcely covered in most texts on the history of our armed forces and is often mentioned in a few lines or described as an action of little importance and without difficulty.
In reality, the invasion of the Kingdom of Albania was a wake-up call and showed all the inefficiency of the Italian Royal Armed Forces in a modern war as the Second World War would later be, which saw the Kingdom of Italy suffer defeat after defeat.
What was supposed to be a 'walk in the park' actually cost the blood of Italian soldiers and sailors, especially in the Durrës area, and only the weakness of the military apparatus of the small Balkan state would not make the Italians pay dearly for the poor organisation of the operation and the logistical problems.
After a description of the pre-1939 events, the book will focus on the stages of the invasion and then move on to a description of the integration of the Albanian armed forces into the Italian ones..

Acknowledgements

This book would never have been written without the help of my friend Arturo Giusti and Paolo Crippa, who kindly allowed me to write for this publishing house.
I would also like to thank Giulio Poggiaroni for his help with the *Regia Marina* and my friend Giorgio for helping me revise the text.

▲ King Zog I in conversation with Galeazzo Ciano during the Italian Foreign Minister's visit to Albania in 1937.

▲ Italian Headquarters on Prefecture Street in Vlora during the First World War.

▼ Albanian troops battery two cannons captured from Italian forces during an attack towards Vlora.

THE END OF WORLD WAR I AND THE WAR OF VALONA

Relations between the Kingdom of Italy and Albania have been close since the birth of the small Balkan state in 1912.
The Treaty of London, signed between Italy and the Entente forces in 1915, provided, in Article 6, for Italian sovereignty over Vlore, the island of Saseno (in Albanian Sazan) and a territory to defend them.
During the First World War, Italian forces were then deployed in Albania to fight the Central Powers and after the end of the conflict much of the country remained in Italian hands. Until 1919, there were no major problems, but gradually the situation began to deteriorate due to the deterioration of the *Albanian Troop Corps*, commanded by General Settimio Piacentini, and nationalist outbreaks in the south of the country, between Gjirokastra and Vlora, fomented by the possibility of a Greek occupation in the region.
In January 1920, an Albanian national congress was convened in Lushnje, which declared the provisional pro-Italian government in Durrës to have fallen. A new government was appointed, based in Tirana, headed by Prime Minister Suleiman bey Delvino, who immediately had the support of the Albanian Gendarmerie, which became his main armed force. However, the Italian situation continued to worsen, mainly due to the lack of the reinforcements wanted by Piacentini, who required at least two brigades; In April, the *Albanian Troop Command* had under its orders the *13th Division* in the north, composed of the *'Udine' Brigade*, the *6th Alpine Regiment*, two mountain artillery batteries and mixed troops, and the *36th* in the south formed by the remnants of the *'Verona'* and *'Puglie'* brigades, three battalions of the *10th Bersaglieri Regiment* and the *LIV Mountain Artillery Group*.
The total number of Italians was around 10,000, an insufficient number that could barely maintain the defensive entrenchment around Vlora; after a short time, the first skirmishes between Albanians and Italians began and in May, the Italian government decided to abandon the hinterland, limiting itself to maintaining only a few coastal areas.
In Vlore, the remnants of three infantry regiments (72nd, 85th and 86th) supported by an artillery battery totalling just 800 men with 34 machine-gun sections were maintained; in the south of the country, protecting Vlore, were the *71st 'Puglie' Infantry Regiment*, stationed between Tepeleni, Gjirokastra and Santi Quaranta and the *10th Bersaglieri Regiment* located between Himara and Port Palermo, totalling just 900 men.
In the north of the country, the Italian occupation was limited to the settlements of San Giovanni di Medua, Alessio and in the centre, Durazzo, maintained by elements of the *'Udine' Brigade*, the *2nd* and *14th Alpine Groups* and artillery units.
In mid-May, the Albanian *Gendarmerie* in Gjirokastra was targeting an insurrection against Tepeleni and Vlora; Piacentini, in response, had the Alpine battalions *'Dronero'*, *'Saluzzo'*, and *'Intra'* land in Vlora, which were already on their way to Italy, creating discontent

among the Italian soldiers but managing to stem the attack of 600 Albanians.

However, the situation did not improve. On 20 May, the Albanian National Defence Committee proclaimed an insurrection against the Italians, managed to gather a few thousand men, and in early June sent an ultimatum to the *Albanian Troop Command*, which was obviously not accepted.

On 5 June, the Albanian attack hit the Italian positions defending Vlora; the Italian units, often isolated and under-staffed, fought as well as they could but were overwhelmed by the Albanians, who captured around 800 men in three days, occupying centres in Vlora's defensive belt (such as Giormi and Quota 115) and overpowering the Italian garrisons in the south of the country; Piacentini ordered the withdrawal of the few remaining troops towards Vlora.

Only after the damage had been done did the Italian government begin to move and it was decided to send the *'Piacenza' Brigade*, the *15th Squadron Autoblindo* and three assault battalions, which caused much protest in Italy from the socialists, who were against the occupation of Albania.

The 1,500-strong *'Piacenza' Brigade* arrived in Vlore on the 9th, improving the situation of the Italian garrison; however, on the same day, the Italians were met with a new ultimatum and the city surrounded by some 5,000 Albanians ready to attack.

The very next day, the Albanian attack began, concentrated mainly in the southern part of the Italian defences, which was repulsed at great cost also thanks to the counter-attack of two Alpine battalions, while an insurrection in the Muslim quarter of Vlora was blocked by the Carabinieri and a ward of military prisoners awaiting trial.

On the 16th, the 1,700 men of the three assault battalions and the *15th Autoblindo Squadron* arrived in Vlore; thus, by the end of June, the Italian garrison in Vlore had more than 5,000 men with 142 machine guns, four armoured cars and 18 cannons.

It was not only the Albanians that affected the Italian troops, but also the malaria that afflicted two-thirds of the Italians guarding the city.

In Italy, protests against sending men to Albania continued and there were also insurrections by Italian soldiers, as in the case of an Arditi unit in Brindisi.

In July, attempts to reach an agreement with the government in Tirana began, thanks to the intervention of Baron Carlo Maria Alberto Aliotti, while the garrison saw the arrival of the *264th Infantry Regiment 'Gaeta'*; on 23 July, 4,000 Albanians attacked the Italian positions but were harshly repulsed.

Finally on 2 August, with the signing of the Tirana Protocol, the Italian occupation of Vlora came to an end and by the end of the month all Italian forces returned home.

▲ Italian and Albanian soldiers near Gjirokastra during the First World War. Source: L'Illustrazione Italiana.

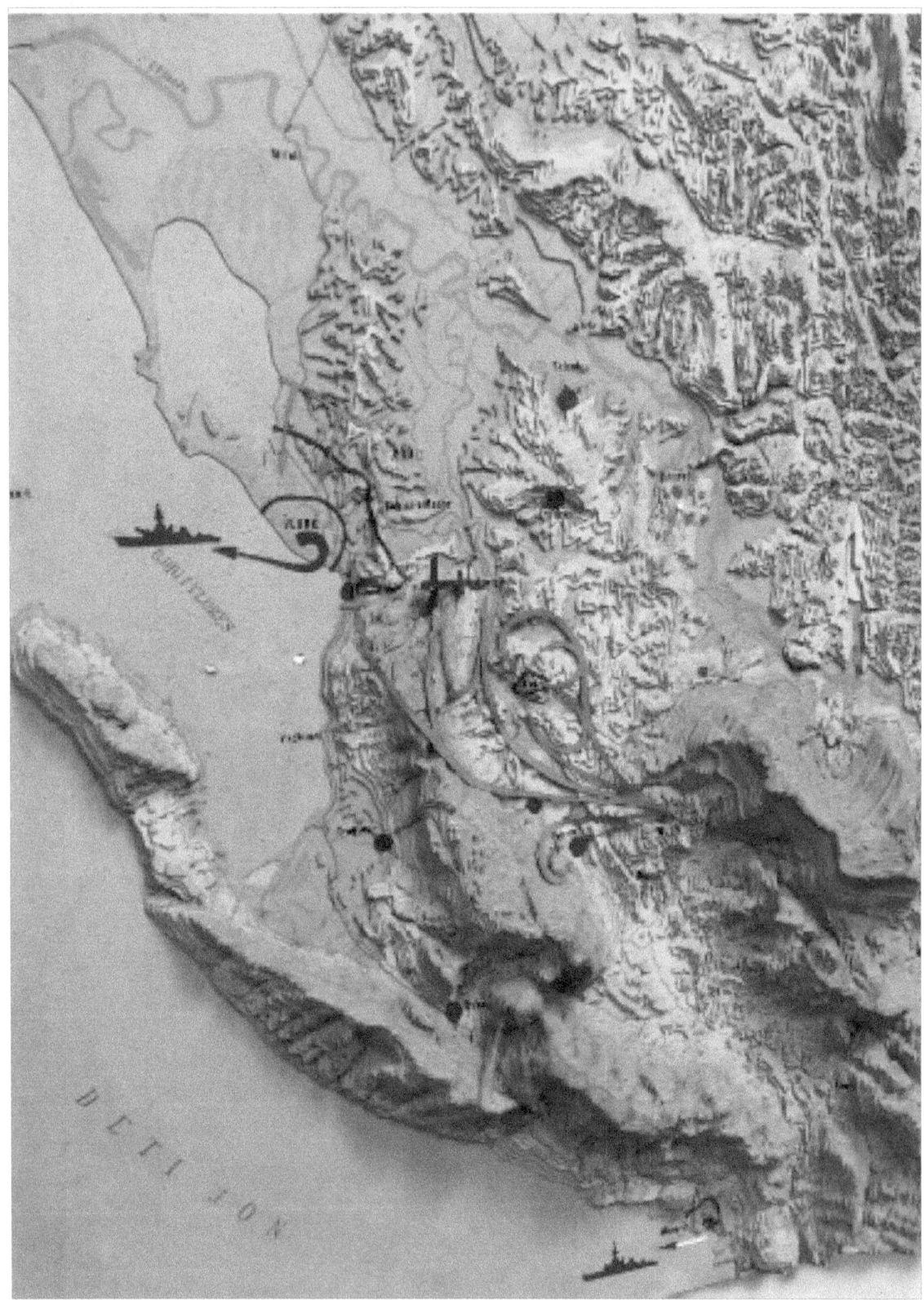

▲ Map of the Albanian attack on Italian positions around Vlora.

RELATIONS BETWEEN THE KINGDOM OF ITALY AND ALBANIA BETWEEN 1920 AND 1939

In October 1920, Albania applied to join the League of Nations and was admitted shortly afterwards. This immediately led the government to a demand for a revision of the borders, also because of an uprising in the north of the country that had led to the birth of the unrecognised Republic of Mirdita, supported by Yugoslavia.

On 9 November 1921, the representatives of Italy, Japan, France and England made two final decisions: Albania was recognised as an independent state and its borders were set, the violation of which was recognised as a 'matter of international importance' and in the event of an attack it would have the support of Italy to preserve its independence.

An inter-allied commission was set up on 18 January 1922, headed by General Enrico Tellini, with the aim of establishing the new Albanian borders, but on 27 August 1923 Tellini was killed by Epirote gangs supported by Greece; the Mussolini government, in response, bombed and occupied the island of Corfu, but the intervention of France and England forced the Duce to withdraw the Italian troops.

The small state had major internal political problems over the years. In December 1921, Ahmed Muhtar Zogolli (the future King Zog I) came to power with the support of the Gendarmerie, but there was strong opposition from the outset, which resulted in an insurrection in June 1924 that brought Bishop Tehofan Stilian Noli, known as Fan Noli, to power, while Zogolli was forced to flee to Belgrade.

The new government, however, was a failure and already in December Zogolli returned to Albania, leading a few thousand armed men, overthrew Fan Noli's government and was appointed president of the republic.

Zogolli immediately increased the efficiency of the *Gendarmerie*, which saw its personnel double, while from the international point of view it began to get very close to Italy thanks to economic agreements and the sending, from the end of 1925, of Italian instructors to the Albanian armed forces, which in 1927 led to the creation of a military mission[1], commanded by Colonel Alberto Pariani, with the aim of reorganising the Albanian armed forces and transforming them into a modern force that was no longer organised into gangs.

The mission wedged itself into all areas of the Albanian armed forces, military schools and pre-military courses were organised, while as far as the organisation of the army was concerned, a number of regiments were immediately formed, under the orders of Italian lieutenant colonels, consisting of three infantry battalions, three artillery batteries and one genius company, and soon afterwards two divisions were also created, whose chiefs of staff

---

1 In 1930, the mission had 163 officers, 42 non-commissioned officers and troops and 2 civilian employees while the Regia Marina sent a small mission to organise the Albanian navy. Taken from *L' Attività Degli Addetti Militari Italiani All'Estero Fra Le Due Guerre Mondiali (1919-1939)*, op. cit. in bibliography.

were also Italian.

The Italians also took an interest in forming a defensive line against a Yugoslav invasion, which was built between Milot and Librazhd with the aim of stemming the enemy attack while waiting for the arrival of Italian forces to reinforce the Albanians.

The small Albanian navy also had an Italian mission, consisting of a few officers and specialists with a few vehicles, while the Gendarmerie was organised by a British mission.

On 1 September 1928, Zogolli proclaimed himself king, with the name of Zog I, and began to distance himself from Italy, which in 1931 led him not to renew the friendship and security pact with it, and from Rome it was decided to withdraw Pariani and replace him with Colonel Riccardo Balocco, who noted how the Italian situation in Albania was deteriorating.

Zog began to move closer to Yugoslavia but could not afford tensions with Italy so, after 1933, he made various economic and military pacts with it, also promising Albanian support in the event of an Italian attack on Yugoslavia.

In 1937, Italian Foreign Minister Galeazzo Ciano visited Tirana and was well received, laying the foundations for various public works programmes. Immediately after the German occupation of Austria in March 1938, Ciano urged Mussolini to occupy the small Balkan state, but the Head of Government postponed the invasion, preferring it to be carried out in collaboration with Yugoslavia.

Indeed, various agreements between Italy and Yugoslavia began and Zog himself began to realise that the situation could deteriorate irretrievably, but the fall of Yugoslavian Prime Minister Milan Stojadinovic eliminated the agreements between Italy and Yugoslavia and forced the former to speed up the timetable for an occupation of Albania, before Yugoslavia gained political strength.

Also creating problems was the German occupation of Bohemia, which, according to Minister Councillor Francesco Jacomoni, led King Zog to consider an attack on Kosovo and to make himself completely available to Italy in the event of an attack on Yugoslavia.

Most probably Zog was bluffing and foresaw an Italian military intervention, on the other hand Mussolini, after having received reassurances from Germany, Hungary, England and Yugoslavia, decided to act and on 25 March a request for annexation to the Kingdom of Italy was sent to King Zog, which was ignored by the Albanian regent.

On 2 April, an ultimatum was issued, which was refused three days later; in the meantime, the Albanian population began to protest against the Italian demands and the Mussolini government decided to repatriate the Italians, including the military mission that returned home on 5 April.

On the 6th, the Italian convoys left for the Albanian coast, while the next day King Zog, instead of uniting the people to resist the Italians, decided to flee to Greece.

▲ Plaque erected in 1939 in memory of General Enrico Tellini, who was killed on 27 August 1923 by an Epirus gang while leading an inter-allied commission sent to Albania to establish borders.

▲ Three officers, followed by a sergeant, land in Corfu on 29 August 1923 with the war flag of the 16th Infantry Regiment. Source: L'Illustrazione Italiana N°36.

▼ Italian boats ready to disembark Italian soldiers on the island of Corfu on 29 August 1923. Source: L'Illustrazione Italiana N°36.

▲ Tehofan Stilian Noli, the man in the centre with the beard, immediately after taking power in Albania in June 1924.

▼ King Zog I, accompanied by a Muslim delegation, reviewing an army division whose soldiers are all armed with Carcano 91.

▲ King Zog I together with his three sisters Myzjen, Ruhije and Maxhide. The uniforms are almost an exact copy of the 1934 model uniform used by Italian officers.

▼ Foreign Minister Galeazzo Ciano visiting Albania while inspecting some Albanian soldiers accompanied by General Xhemal Aranitasi [left], commander of the Albanian army.

THE ITALIAN INVASION PLAN

The Italian invasion plan had already been studied for some time by the *Regio Esercito General Staff* and the mobilisation of the units assigned to the expeditionary corps would not have been a big problem, but the government did not allow sufficient time for optimal organisation and the *Regio Esercito* was forced to mobilise units made up of training units that had the serious problem of being poorly cohesive.

On 13 March, the Chief of Staff of the Regio Esercito, Alberto Pariani, described the plan to Mussolini, Jacomoni and Ciano, pointing out that the command of the expeditionary corps would be entrusted to General Alfredo Guzzoni, who at the time was still in the dark as he was only informed of this on 31 March.

At the beginning of April, the expeditionary *corps*, called the *Tirana Overseas Expeditionary Corps (OMT), was* organised. It was divided into three groups with a total of 22,000 men, 64 cannons, 125 CV 35 tanks, 860 vehicles, 1,200 motorbikes, 5,500 bicycles and 2,500 quadrupeds.

The *I Scaglione, which was* the only one that actually took part in the invasion, was divided into four columns with different target locations:

- *Scattini Column*: Under the command of Colonel Arturo Scattini, it was to land at St. John of Medua ('Shëngjin' in Albanian) and had Devoli and Vlora as its targets;

  The column consisted of a regiment of Bersaglieri, formed by the *3rd*, *6th* and *28th Battalions*, half a battalion of the *'San Marco' Marine Infantry Regiment*, an R.4 radio section[2], two radio stations (one R.4A[3] and one R.O.C[4].) and a car workshop;

- *Messe Column*: Under the command of General Giovanni Messe, it was to land in Durres and advance on Tirana and Coriza. The column consisted of the *Bersaglieri Regiment* 'Sozzani'[5], formed by the *2nd*, *14th* and *17th Battalions*, the *Formation Regiment 'Mannerini'*[6], composed of the *1st* and *2nd Battalions* and a 65/17 battery of the *3rd Regiment 'Granatieri di Sardegna'*, the *Tactical Group 'Anderson'*[7] consisting of the *VII* and *XI Bersaglieri Battalions*, the *'D'Antoni' Assault Tank Group*[8], consisting of the *VIII* and *X L Tank Battalions* with 31 CV 35 tanks, the *I Battalion* of the *47th Infantry Regiment 'Ferrara'*, a 20 mm battery of the *23rd Infantry Division 'Murge'*[9], two R radio sections, by three radio

---

2 Somatic radio station intended for the *Radiotelegraph Sections* of infantry divisions and express divisions. Taken from www.angetmi.it.
3 Entered into service in 1934, it was a radio transmitter and receiver intended for communication between Large Unit commands and aircraft in flight. Taken from www.angetmi.it.
4 Developed in 1935 for colonial units, its purpose was to link unit commands.
5 Commanded by Colonel Nino Sozzani.
6 Commanded by Colonel Alberto Mannerini.
7 Commanded by Colonel Amerigo Anderson.
8 Commanded by Colonel Giovanni D'Antoni.
9 Formed in March 1939 and composed of the *47th* and *48th* Infantry Regiments and the *14th* Artillery Regiment. The division was renamed *23rd Infantry Division 'Ferrara'* on 24 May of the same year. Taken from *L'esercito e i suoi corpi*, op. cit. in bibliography.

stations (one R.4A and two R.O.C.) and by an auto workshop;

- *Bernardi Column*: Commanded by Colonel Tullio Bernardi, it targeted the Fieri area after landing in Vlora.

   It consisted of a Bersaglieri regiment, made up of the *I* and *XVI Battalions*, the *XL* and *LXXVI Black Shirts Battalions*, two radio stations (one R.4A and one R.O.C.) and a car workshop;

- *Carasi Column*: Under the orders of Colonel Mario Carasi, it targeted Devoli and Gjirokastra after landing at Santi Quaranta ('<u>Saranda'</u> in Albanian).

   The column consisted of a Bersaglieri regiment, strengthened by the *20th* and *23rd Battalions*, the *3rd Gruppo Squadroni Carri Veloci 'San Giorgio'*, half a battalion of the *Reggimento Infantteria di Marina 'San Marco'*, an R.4 radio section, two radio stations (one R.4A and one R.O.C.) and a car workshop.

The total strength of the *I Scaglione* was 10,400 non-commissioned officers and troops and 560 officers, the *San Marco* battalion and the two Black Shirts battalions are not included in the count.[10]

After the occupation of the town, the next two groups would disembark, the *II* consisting of a battalion of the *23rd 'Murge' Infantry Division*, the *Provisional Cavalry Regiment* (made up of two tank squadron groups), a garrison infantry company two Engineer companies and three Artillery Groups, while *III* was formed by the *23rd Infantry Division 'Murge'* and the *'Peano' Black Shirts Battalion Group*, with four battalions (*XCII, CXI, CII* and *CLII*).

Several convoys were organised to transport the Expeditionary Corps from Taranto, Brindisi and Bari; the *Regia Marina* deployed a large force for the operation under the command of Admiral Arturo Riccardi, which was divided into four groups[11].

The *First Group,* under the command of Divisional Admiral Angelo Iachino, had San Giovanni di Medua as its target and was equipped with a light cruiser (*Giovanni dalle Bande Nere*), three destroyers (*Da Recco, Folgore* and *Fulmine*), two torpedo boats (*Pleiadi* and *Polluce*), a tanker (*Garigliano*) and a motor ship (*Umbria*).

The *Second Group,* targeting Durazzo, was commanded by Rear-Admiral Sportello and had three heavy cruisers (*Gorizia, Pola* and *Zara*), four torpedo boats (*Libra, Lince, Lira* and *Lupo*), a seaplane carrier (*Giuseppe Miraglia*), a repair ship (*Quarnaro*), two tankers (*Adige* and *Tirso*), two motor ships (*Adriatico, Barletta*) and four steamers (*Argentaro, Palatino, Toscana* and *Valsavoia*).

The *Third Group,* commanded by Lieutenant Admiral Arturo Ricciardi, was targeting Valona and consisted of two battleships (*Conte di Cavour* and *Giulio Cesare*), four destroyers

---

10 The *San Marco* battalion had a strength of 664 men while the Black Shirts had 1,500 men. Taken from *Diario Storico del Comando Supremo Volume I Tomo 2*, op. cit. in bibliography.
11 They are not counted in the list but there were also three MAS [Motoscafo Armato Silurante]. Taken from *La Regia Marina tra le due guerre mondiali,* op. cit. in bibliography.

(*Grecale*, *Libeccio*, *Saetta* and *Scirocco*), four torpedo boats (*Castor*, *Centaurus*, *Cigno* and *Climene*), a minelayer (*Azio*), a tanker (*Isonzo*) and a steamer (*Sannio*).

The *Fourth Group was* aimed at Santi Quaranta under the orders of Division Admiral Oscar di Giamberardino and had two light cruisers (*Duca degli Abruzzi* and *Giuseppe Garibaldi*), two destroyers (*Baleno* and *Freccia*), four torpedo boats (*Airone*, *Alcione*, *Aretusa* and *Ariel*), three tankers (*Garda*, *Sesia* and *Scrivia*), a steamer (*Asmara*) and a motor vessel (*Marin Sanudo*).

The *Regia Marina*'s task was to escort convoys and provide support from the coast to advancing columns.

The *Regia Aeronautica* for the invasion mobilised the *'A' Squadron* from elements of the *2nd Air Force* and placed it under the command of Air Force General Francesco Pricolo, former commander of the *2nd Territorial Air Zone* and the *2nd Air Force*.

The *'A' Squadron*, stationed at various Apulian airports, had a total of 350 aircraft divided into a *Bombardment Division*[12], a mixed one with fighters and bombers[13], a *Transport Division*[14], the *28th T Wing*, a civil Wing[15], the *35th Maritime Bombardment Wing* and the *42nd Air Observation Squadron*.

The purpose of these air units, in addition to supporting the army columns, was to transport the two Grenadier battalions and possibly other troops and supplies, while the *42nd Air Observation Squadron* was to ensure connections between the various advancing columns.

---

12 Formed by the *11th* and *12th Stormo*. Taken from *La Regia Aeronautica 1939-1943*…,op. cit in bibliography.
13 Formed by the *6th Terrestrial Fighter Wing*, *30th* and *36th Terrestrial Bombardment Wing*. Taken from *La Regia Aeronautica 1939-1943*…,op. cit in bibliography.
14 Formed by the *33rd* and *34th Terrestrial Bombardment Wing*. Taken from *La Regia Aeronautica 1939-1943*…,op. cit in bibliography.
15 Made up of 40 aircraft of the airlines *Linee Aeree Transcontinentali Italiane*, *Ala Littoria* and *Aviolinee Italiane*. Taken from *La Regia Aeronautica 1939-1943*…,op. cit in bibliography.

▲ General Alfredo Guzzoni.

▲ Giovanni Messe, commander of the Messe Column, visiting some Bersaglieri deployed on the Russian front in 1942. Source ACS.

▼ The battleship *Andrea Doria* at sea during some naval manoeuvres.

▲ Beautiful photo of the heavy cruiser *Zara* as it opens fire with its 203 mm guns at an enemy naval formation during World War II.

▼ Seaplane carrier *Giuseppe Miraglia* in a 1930s photograph.

▲ Air Force General Francesco Pricolo (right) in conversation with Italian pilots during the Battle of the Western Alps in June 1940. Source ACS.

▲ Soldiers of the Albanian army during a review. Note the completely Italian armament and equipment as well as the clothing, which closely resembles Italian clothing.

THE ALBANIAN ARMED FORCES AND THE DEFENCE PLAN

The Albanian army (in Albanian <u>Ushtria Mbretërore Shqiptare</u>) in April 1939 was commanded by General Xhemal Aranitasi who, however, fled on the eve of the Italian invasion and the command passed to Colonel Prenk Pervizi, later commander of the Albanian partisans during World War II.

The army had a strength of about 15,000 men, but on the eve of the invasion, the number of armed men was only 8,000, while the armament was purely Italian and had 23,000 Carcano rifles, 6,000 Austro-Hungarian rifles, 60 FIAT machine guns and 18 Schwarzlose[16].

The availability of ammunition was very low and could only allow a maximum of three days of fire.

The Albanian army was divided into three arms; the Infantry (in Albanian, <u>Armët e Këmbsorisë</u>) consisted of seven infantry battalions, each consisting of three infantry companies and one machine-gun company with a total strength of about 500 men.

The Artillery (in Albanian <u>Armët and Artilerisë</u>) had thirteen mountain artillery batteries, nine armed with 65 mm Model 1913[17] guns and four with 75 mm Skoda howitzers[18] and two country artillery batteries[19], each with four 75/27 Model 1906 guns[20].

To these must be added the *Prandaj* coastal battery defending Durres, commanded by Captain Gjergj Mosko and consisting of four 75/27 guns, and two other mountain batteries operating with the *Gendarmerie* and the *Royal Guard* respectively. It also had an embryonic anti-aircraft artillery, which in April 1939 could only count on a few machine guns.

The Corps of Engineers (in Albanian <u>Armët and Xhenios</u>) consisted of three battalions of sappers and a few units of transmissions, while for transport, the army had an autorepartement with about 500 vehicles, light and heavy trucks.

There was a minimal presence of armoured vehicles, all grouped in a squadron located in Tirana that had two FIAT 3000 tanks, six CV 33 tanks, six Lancia 1ZM armoured cars and two Bianchi armoured cars.

All these branches of the army had the presence of Italian training officers and, most probably, these affected the spirit of resistance of the Albanian soldiers.

---

16 To these machine guns must be added 12 FIATs and 24 Schwarzlose assigned to the *Gendarmerie*. Taken from http://www.niehorster.org/042_albania/Albania.htm.
17 It entered service as mountain artillery in the *Regio Esercito* in 1913 as Cannone da 65A [Steel]; in the 1930s it equipped the accompanying batteries of Italian infantry regiments as Cannone da 65/17, remaining in service until the end of World War II. Taken from *Guida alle artiglierie italiane nella 2ª Guerra Mondiale*, op. cit. in bibliography.
18 The howitzers were the 7.5 cm Skoda Gebirgskanone M.15, used by the Austro-Hungarian mountain artillery. These after the war also entered service in the *Regio Esercito* with 75/13 Model 1915 howitzers, remaining in service with the Alpine artillery until the end of the Second World War. Taken from *Guida alle artiglierie italiane nella 2ª Guerra Mondiale*, op. cit. in bibliography.
19 Officially one was hippotrained and one self-propelled. Taken from *The Albanian Units in World War II,* op. cit. in bibliography.
20 A piece that entered service in the *Regio Esercito* in 1906 and was also used in World War II as the cannon of the divisional artillery regiments. Taken from *Guida alle artiglierie italiane nella 2ª Guerra Mondiale*, op. cit. in bibliography.

Also included in the army was the *Gendarmerie* (in Albanian Arma e Xhandarmërisë), the only branch without Italian influence but trained by a British mission, which in April 1939 had about 3,800 personnel divided into six battalions, each equipped with four Schwarzlose machine guns with the exception of the Burrel *Instruction Battalion*, which had 12 FIAT machine guns and a mountain artillery battery with four Skoda howitzers.

There was also the *Border Guard* (in Albanian Roja Mbretnore and Kufinit) with a force of about 1,800 men divided into 14 companies with police duties similar to the Italian *Royal Guardia di Finanza*.

Finally, the *Royal Guard* (in Albanian: Garda Mbretërore) consisted of 926 men divided into five infantry companies, a mountain artillery battery (with four 75 mm Skoda howitzers), a cavalry squadron and a band.

In the event of conflict, the Albanian army also had at its disposal volunteer reservists divided into 10 battalions, totalling about 8,000 men, who performed auxiliary tasks or were integrated into army units.

The Albanian defences were intended to hold out as long as possible in anticipation of a possible Yugoslav intervention and were structured on four defensive lines - more in name than in fact - defending the capital Tirana; the army forces were divided into four defensive sectors and the garrison in Durres.

The four defensive sectors were composed as follows:

- *I Sector*: Under the orders of Lieutenant Colonel Shaban Bega, it covered the sector between Milot and the Shkumbin River with the infantry battalions *Deja*, *Dajti* and *Korata*, two mountain artillery batteries (with four Italian 65 mm cannons), one company of the hoe genius and 100 reservists;

- *Sector II*: covered the sector between Milot and Shkodra and consisted of the infantry battalions *Gramos* and *Tarabosh*, a battalion of the *Gendarmerie*, two mountain artillery batteries (four 65 mm cannons) and 500 reservists under the command of Lieutenant Colonel Kucuk Valagaj;

- *Sector III*: Under the orders of Lieutenant Colonel Faik Cuku garrisoned the Shkumbin River Vjose line and had the *Tomori* and *Kaptina* infantry battalions, a *Gendarmerie* battalion, two mountain artillery batteries (four 65 mm cannons) and 800 conscripts;

- *Sector IV*: Commanded by Lieutenant Colonel Ali Riza Topalli, it garrisoned the Santi Quaranta area with two battalions of the *Border Guard*, a battalion of the *Gendarmerie* and 800 conscripts;

- *Durrës Garrison*: Under the command of Major Abaz Kupi, consisting of a *Border Guard battalion*, a Gendarmerie battalion, a mountain artillery battery (2 Skoda 75 mm howitzers), a coastal battery (4 75/27 Model 1906 guns), a sailor platoon and 800 conscripts.

▲ Albanian officers and troops during a military review. Note the Albanian war flag.

The Albanian navy was a tiny affair under the orders of an Italian commander, Lieutenant Commander Taddei; it numbered just over 150 personnel divided between four harbour master's offices and a flotilla with only four ELCO-type MAS[21] delivered to Albania in 1928. *The Tirane* class MAS were armed with a 76 mm cannon and two machine guns and were stationed at the Durazzo base.

The only other ship available was the royal yacht *Illirja*[22], given by Italy to King Zog in 1938 as a wedding gift.

The Albanian army also had at its disposal a minimal air force of which, however, very little is known; some sources state that in the 1920s Albania received five Albatros L.47s, the civil version of the Albatros CXV[23]. Both the News Chronicle, in an article of 8 April 1939, and The Time on 17 April stated Albanian possession of only two aircraft but there is no further data to ascertain the veracity of these or other sources.

▲ The Albanian army's 75/27 truck battery. The trucks are FIAT 15ter.

---

21 The four MAS were named after Albanian cities: *Durres, Saranda, Tirane* and *Vlore*. Taken from https://naval-encyclopedia.com/ww2/minor-navies.php#al.

22 Until 1935, the Albanian Navy also had two minesweepers, *Skënderbeg* and *Shqiperi*, former German *FM-class* minesweepers received in 1925. By 1939, the two vessels were no longer active. Taken from https://www.lavocedelmarinaio.com.

23 The German civil registry marks five Albatros CXV/L47 with registration codes D-140, D-185, D-186, D-300 and D-586 without indicating the customer. Perhaps they were sent to Albania but we have no further information. Taken from http://www.airhistory.org.uk/gy/reg_D-1.html.

▲ Another photo of the 75/27 tank battery during a parade. All soldiers are equipped with Adrian helmets while the armament consists of Carcano 91 rifles for T.S. [Special Troops].

▼ A unit of the Albanian army, led by an officer, during a parade in front of King Zog. The photo shows the clear reference to the Italian uniforms and equipment of officers and troops. Source: *Albanian units in World War II* - Luigi Manes.

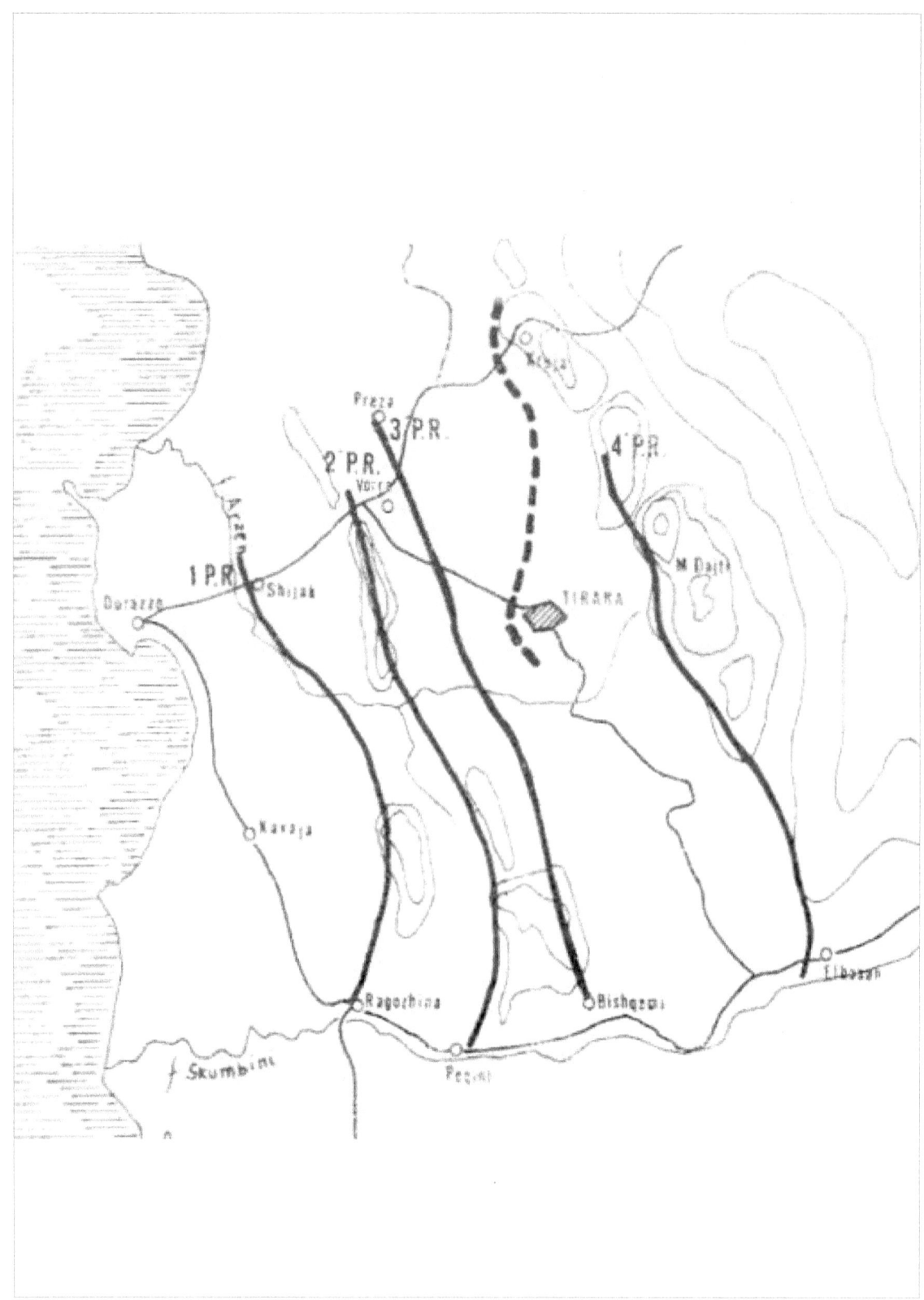

▲ The four Albanian defence lines defending the capital Tirana. Source USSME.

▲ Two FIAT 3000 tanks immediately after their capture by the Italians in Tirana.

▲ King Zog, accompanied by senior officers, inspects a Carcano 91 belonging to an Albanian soldier during a review.

▼ Albanian soldiers talking with some Albanian civilians, most probably during the Italian occupation. Source: L'Illustrazione Italiana N°26.

▲ A group of Albanian gendarmes photographed in the 1930s.

▼ The MAS *Saranda* and *Vlora* in the port of Durres in 1936.

THE LANDING AND OCCUPATION OF ALBANIA

The embarkation of men and vehicles began on 6 April at the ports of Taranto and Brindisi and at 11 o'clock of the same day, due to the slowness of some steamships, the convoys bound for Vlora and Santi Quaranta left, while those for Durrës and San Giovanni di Medua left at 6.30 p.m. The objective was to land at all ports at the same time at 4.30 a.m. on 7 April, but due to various delays, the Italian troops were taken ashore well after the appointed time.

- *Bernardi Column*

A landing company[24] of the *Regia Marina* disembarked in Vlora only at 6.30 a.m. and was immediately hit by fire from some of the *Gendarmerie* units stationed in the Albanian port, which were silenced thanks to the intervention of the Bersaglieri and an Italian destroyer, allowing the Italians to establish a bridgehead.
Immediately afterwards, the two Black Shirts battalions also landed, which were targeted by machine guns in the city's archaeological museum, then quickly silenced by the intervention of Italian soldiers.
After the occupation of Vlora, the Black Shirts remained garrisoned in the city while the two Bersaglieri battalions began to advance towards Fieri, arriving in the early afternoon near the heights of Bestrova, eight kilometres from Vlora, where an Albanian battalion from Elbasan was stationed.
The report by General Guzzoni states that this battalion was called *Semani* and was 700 men strong and some artillery; in reality, there was no Albanian infantry battalion named by that name but only a mountain artillery battery, with two 65 mm cannons, probably reinforced by the Elbasan *Gendarmerie* battalion, 400 men strong and four machine guns.
The Italian attack on these positions was supported by 320 mm artillery fire from the battleship *Conte di Cavour* and after three hours the Albanians were dislodged from their positions at the cost of three Italian casualties.
As evening approached, the Italian advance was halted and resumed on the 8th at 5 a.m.; the Italian units overran the few Albanian rearguards and by 6 p.m. occupied Fieri. On the 9th, without encountering resistance, the Bersaglieri entered Berat after a 120 km march.

- *Carasi Column*

The column took land at Santi Quaranta and, after quickly suppressing the slight resistance of the *Gendarmerie* at the cost of one dead sailor and two wounded Bersaglieri, established a bridgehead in the coastal town, leaving two companies of the *San Marco* to garrison there and sending the Bersaglieri with the *3rd Group 'San Giorgio' Squadron* towards Delvino.

---

24 The landing companies of the *Regia Marina* consisted of sailors from a ship who were armed with rifles and machine guns.

The city was occupied the same day without encountering resistance.
The next day, Italian troops advanced towards Gjirokastra, occupying it on 9 April without any problems except for the poor state of the Albanian roads.

- *Column Masses*

The first ships of the convoy arrived at the port of Durrës at 4.50 a.m. and found the city fully illuminated, and at 5 a.m. the torpedo boat *Lupo*, followed by two other torpedo boats, entered the port of Durrës carrying some sailors from the landing companies.

At 5.25 a.m., Guzzoni ordered disembarkation, but the situation was not the best because the steamer *Palatino*, carrying the *XXVII Bersaglieri Battalion*, had not yet arrived; the steamer *Toscana* could not penetrate the harbour because of the shallow water; and the seaplane carrier *Giuseppe Miraglia*, carrying the tanks of the *D'Antoni Regiment*, could not dock because the dock was occupied by the steamer *Aquitania*, which was due to arrive later.

In the meantime, the landing companies had disembarked and were immediately hit by heavy fire from the buildings surrounding the port and to support the action, the Italians had to land the *1st Battalion* of the *47th Infantry Regiment 'Ferrara'*.

In the meantime, the Albanian fire did not stop and commendable was the action of the naval petty officer Mujo Ulqinaku who gathered a group of Albanian sailors and, with a machine gun, continued to fire on the Italian troops until he was killed by a shell fired by the Italian torpedo boats that started firing towards the Albanian positions at 6 o'clock.

Immediately after the bombardment, the *'Anderson' Tactical Group* landed and, together with the *I Battalion* of the *'Ferrara'*, began to advance into the settlement to silence the resistance of the Albanian troops, composed mostly of gendarmes and supported by two artillery batteries.

By around 9 a.m., the city of Durrës had been occupied by the Italians, but enemy resistance continued on the surrounding heights and General Messe called for cruiser fire to hit the area of Rasbul and Kavaja, where there was an artillery battery, most probably the *Drin Battery*, which was attempting to hit the Italian ships in the harbour.

At 10 a.m., General Guzzoni went ashore to hold discussions with some Albanian parliamentarians - Economy Minister Rrock Gera, Foreign Minister Libohova and Lieutenant Colonel Semik Koka - who proposed a collaboration between Albanians and Italians and demanded the deployment of an Italian infantry division in Albania under the orders of King Zog and that Guzzoni interrupt the Italian operations.

The Italian general, irritated, demanded the withdrawal of the Albanian troops, but was not too aggressive because the Italian units in Durrës numbered only one efficient battalion, while the rest of the troops were still disembarking and the tanks had not yet come ashore. Added to this, Colonel Manlio Gabrielli, the Italian military attaché in Albania, reported the presence of a force of about 4-5,000 Albanians under the king's orders ready to attack the Italian right flank.

These forces were imaginary, but Guzzoni, although sceptical, could not know this, so he agreed with the parliamentarians to reappear at 3 p.m. and, if not, the Italian advance would restart at 4 p.m.

Guzzoni did not want to accept the agreement, mainly because of the clause that placed Italian units under the Albanian king, and continued to land troops in the port of Durrës, including the CV 35 tanks that had been landed since 1 p.m.

At 3 p.m., no MPs showed up and five minutes before 4 p.m., the Albanians blew up the bridge over the Arzen river; immediately Guzzoni sent the *Bersaglieri Regiment 'Sozzani'* to Shijak to occupy the other bridge over the river but had to block further advances because some Italian units were still disembarking.

Throughout the day, the Italians had eight sailors and two infantrymen killed and 46 sailors, infantrymen and Bersaglieri wounded.

At dawn on the 8th, the Italian advance began again and Sozzani's Bersaglieri advanced towards Vorra, where there was an Albanian contingent, but they were slowed down by the actions of some enemy nuclei and by 7.30 the Italian column had advanced a few kilometres while Vorra was bombed by the *Regia Aeronautica*.

Another problem affected the *Messe Column*; drums of diesel instead of petrol had been landed during the night and this forced the Italian tanks and trucks to remain stationed in Durres, slowing down the Italian advance even more.

Because of this mistake, Messe and Guzzoni ordered the Bersaglieri to advance anyway, regardless of enemy fire, and it was not until 8:30 that they received support from a tank battalion and a motorbike company. This motorised column was ordered by Messe to advance quickly on Tirana and immediately the *Gendarmerie* positions between Vorra and Kashari were attacked. The Italian motorised units, supported by the *XXVII Bersaglieri Battalion* and a motorbike company from the north, surprised the Albanian gendarmes who surrendered without a fight and at 9.30 a.m. the Italians entered Tirana while at 10 a.m. the two airborne Grenadier battalions began to disembark at the city's airport.

Immediately after entering the city, Colonel D'Antoni was ordered to advance towards Elbasan with a column consisting of the *10th Tank Battalion* and the *14th and 17th Bersaglieri Battalions*; the column left the Albanian capital at 4 p.m. and reached Qafa and Krrabes at 6.30 p.m. where it captured without a fight the Albanian troops[25] under the command of King Zog's nephew, Prince Hjssein Dolshisti, reaching Elbasan at 8.30 p.m.

The objectives of the *Messe Column* had been achieved and on the 9th the Italian troops consolidated the positions they had reached.

- *Scattini Column*

At 5.30 a.m., a company of the *San Marco* began to land at San Giovanni di Medua, which was immediately targeted by machine-gun fire, which was immediately silenced by the guns of two destroyers, and the town was occupied within half an hour.

Immediately afterwards, the Bersaglieri regiment landed, allowing Colonel Scattini to send the *XXVIII Bersaglieri Battalion* towards Alessio (Lezhe in Albanian); immediately outside San Giovanni di Medua the battalion encountered stiff resistance, estimated by Italian re-

---

25 The Italian documents state the capture of two batteries of somatic artillery, many individual weapons, a lot of ammunition and materials of the Engineer Corps. Taken from *Report on Military Action in Albania on 7, 8 and 9 April 1939* in *Diario Storico del Comando Supremo Volume I Tomo 2*, op. cit. in bibliography.

ports at 150 men, which forced the unit to halt. The Italians resumed the attack, driving the Albanians back across the Drin river, and occupied Alessio at 14:30.

Immediately after the occupation of the city, the *3rd* and *6th Bersaglieri Battalions* set out from St. John of Medua with Shkodra as their objective; the column advanced slowly due to the poor state of the roads, but was blocked by Albanian resistance in Bushat, carried by elements of the *Gendarmerie* (in Shkodra it had a battalion with 400 men and 4 machine guns) and mixed elements of the *2nd* Albanian *Sector*.

The next day at dawn, the *3rd* and *6th Bersaglieri Battalions* overcame resistance and began to advance towards Shkodra, but were blocked by strong resistance near Drinassa, which was supported by the 65 mm guns of the two mountain artillery batteries of *Sector II*. Albanian resistance was fierce and an Italian attack was repulsed, resulting in the death of Lieutenant Riccardo Bombig[26] of the *3rd Battalion*; it was not until 1.30 p.m. that the Italian Consul in Shkodra arrived at the Italian troops and announced the surrender of the city and the withdrawal of the Albanian forces. To the south, a company of the *XXVIII Bersaglieri Battalion* was sent to Vorra in support of the *Messe Column,* following it to Tirana where it remained until the end of operations.

THE ACTIONS OF THE REGIA AERONAUTICA

The employment of the *'A' Squadron* during the occupation of Albania was very limited; on 7 April, there were a few reconnaissance flights by aircraft of the *35th Maritime Bombardment Wing* and the *36th Land Bombardment Wing*, while the only bombing action was carried out on 8 April by a few S.M. 79s of the *108th Land Bombardment Group* against the village of Vorra, where enemy resistance had been reported.

On the ninth day, some reconnaissance was carried out by S.M. 79 of the *12th Terrestrial Bombardment Wing*, while the following day, a large part of the *'A' Squadron* reached Albania and in Tirana airport alone there were 80 aircraft, which created logistical problems also due to the lack of aviation fuel.

Italian fighter actions were limited to escorting bombers and aircraft flown by various generals of the *Regia Aeronautica.*

Precisely with regard to them, there were a series of individual actions that were more propagandistic than military; on the 7th and 8th, General Giuseppe Valle carried out two reconnaissance missions, one between San Giovanni di Medua and Shkodra and the other towards Durres, in a Savoia Marchetti S.M. 79, claiming not to have noticed any major movements of enemy units.

On 8 April, an S.M. 79, piloted by General Ferruccio Ranza, the other Savoia-Marchetti of General Valle and, at 10 o'clock, the S.M. 81, carrying the two battalions of the *3rd 'Grenadieri di Sardegna' Regiment*, arrived at Tirana airport.

---

26 He was decorated with the Gold Medal for Military Valour with the following motivation: *Commander of an advanced company, already distinguished in the previous landing operation, with exceptional calm and serene disregard for danger, he kept his bersaglieri firmly in place when they were being hit by violent fire. In order to attempt to cross a bridge, which was mined and partly broken, he dared to do so at the head of a few brave men. In his heroic attempt, he was mortally wounded by a machine gun barrage: an admirable example of a high sense of duty and personal valour.* Taken from http://decoratialvalormilitare.istitutonastroazzurro.org/#.

On the 10th, General Francesco Pricolo landed with an S.M. 79 on the airport of Coriza (Korca in Albanian) and received the surrender of the Albanian garrison.

In the end, the main task of the *Regia Aeronautica* during the operations in Albania was to launch leaflets to the civilian population calling for calm and cooperation with the Italians. On 15 April, the *'A' Squadron* was disbanded, renaming it the *'Albania' Mixed Division* and placing it under the command of General Vincenzo Velardi; in the following days, a number of units that took part in the action were disbanded and the civil aircraft were returned to their respective air companies.

▲ The torpedo boat *Libra* in the port of Durres.

▲ Light tank of the *Raggruppamento Carri d'Assalto D'Antoni* while being disembarked in the port of Durres by the seaplane carrier *Giuseppe Miraglia*.

▼ Light tanks embarked in the port of Brindisi to be sent to Albania. Source: courtesy of Paolo Crippa.

▲ Some of the light tanks just disembarked from the *Giuseppe Miraglia*.
▼ A CV 35 of the *D'Antoni Assault Tank Regiment as it* disembarks in the port of Durres from the seaplane carrier *Giuseppe Miraglia*. Source Benvenuti - Colonna.

▲ A light tank intends to descend from the *Giuseppe Miraglia* seaplane port on 7 April. Source: courtesy of Paolo Crippa.

▼ Italian soldiers waiting to disembark in Durres. Note the great heterogeneity of the helmets, which are both the M33 model and the old M15 and M16.

▲ Italian trucks enter the city of Tirana, previously occupied by the Italian military.

▼ Italian units, supported by the light tanks, entered Durres without encountering much resistance. Source Benvenuti - Colonna.

▲ An Italian sailor from the landing companies escorts two Albanian civilians (most probably volunteers from the Albanian army) while a column of Bersaglieri cyclists is passing by.

▼ Beautiful photo of an Italian torpedo boat in the port of Durres while a column of Bersaglieri cyclists passes in the background.

▲ Propaganda photograph showing the Grenadiers of the *'Mannerini' Training Regiment, who have* just arrived at Tirana airport, greeted festively by the civilian population. Two Savoia-Marchetti S.M. 81 can be seen in the background.

▼ Grenadiers ready to depart from Tirana airport with a Breda Ba.44 from *Ala Littoria* towards another Albanian city.

▲ A column of light tanks passing through Tirana.

▼ Two light tanks pass in front of the headquarters of the Bank of Naples in Durres accompanied by some Italian soldiers. Source Benvenuti - Colonna.

▲ Light tanks were the first to cross the city of Tirana during the occupation of the Albanian capital. Source Benvenuti - Colonna.

▲ A column of light tanks passes through a small Albanian village to the indifference of the civilian population. Source Paolo Crippa.

▲ OM truck being disembarked in an Albanian port.

▲ Grenadiers of the *'Mannerini' Training Regiment* intent on talking to the Albanian civilian population. Source: Niccolò Lucarelli - Italians in Albania 1939 1945 - Delta Editrice.

▼ Issue of the *Corriere della Sera* of 8 April 1939 announcing the entry of Italian troops into Tirana.

CORRIERE DELLA SERA

PER LA DIFESA DELLA PACE E DEGLI INTERESSI ITALIANI NELL'ADRIATICO

Le nostre truppe entrate a Tirana
La capitale albanese occupata stamane alle 9.30

La ignominiosa fuga di Zog e del suo Governo - La Legazione d'Italia saldo fortilizio in mezzo alla furia brigantesca

La Spagna firma il Patto anticomintern

Pax adriatica

I criminali liberati e armati da Zog

Appello agli albanesi

▲ Light tanks of the *D'Antoni Assault Tank Regiment* pass through the city of Tirana observed by the Albanian population. Source Benvenuti - Colonna.

THE ARRIVAL OF THE OTHER SCALES AND NEW DIVISIONS

In the days following the occupation, both the *2nd* and *3rd Scaglione* arrived and among these units was the *Provisional Cavalry Regiment,* under the command of Colonel Raffaele Pelligra, made up of the *1st Squadron Group* of the *'Lancieri di Aosta' Regiment*, the *2nd Squadron Group of* the *'Genova Cavalry'* Regiment, a machine-gun platoon of the *'Genova Cavalry' Regiment* and the Command.
The *Provisional Cavalry Regiment* landed in Durrës as part of the *2nd Escalade* on 14 April and deployed near Devoli and Fieri before being divided into two columns with the aim of reaching Peshkopi.
The *I Squadron Group* passed through Tirana, Alessio and Shkodra, and finally arrived in Peshkopi.
The *2nd Squadron Group* initially descended towards the south of Albania, reaching Berat and Permet, and then headed north, skirting the border with Greece and Yugoslavia, and finally reaching Peshkopi.
New units were immediately sent to guard the newly occupied territory, on 15 April the *3rd Alpine Division 'Julia'* left Bari and was stationed in Scutari, on the 18th from Brindisi the *7th Infantry Division 'Lupi di Toscana'* took up position between Korca and Pogradec while on the 25th the *19th. Infantry Division 'Venezia'* landed in Durres and was assigned to guard the area between Elbasan and Pogradec. The *23rd Infantry Division 'Murge'*, which reached full strength with the *3rd Scaglione*, was stationed between Santi Quaranta, Premeti and Gjirokastra.

▲ A platoon of light tanks of the *31st Carrista Infantry Regiment* during the Durazzo parade on 24 April 1939. Source Benvenuti - Column.

▼ A column of light tanks and *Bersaglieri* motorcyclists of the *2nd Bersaglieri Regiment* parade on 24 April 1939 in Durres. Source Benvenuti - Column.

▲ Lance Corporal of the *19th Infantry Division 'Venezia'* photographed in Albania in September 1940. Note the Lion of St. Mark on his chest, a badge worn by members of the division. Collection of the author.

▲ Tanks and soldiers of the *31st Carrista Infantry Regiment* deployed in Scanderbeg Square during Emilio De Bono's visit in the spring of 1940. Source: Ratti Archives.

▼ L tanks, followed by some Bersaglieri on a Guzzi Trialce, advance into Greek territory in the first days of the war against the Kingdom of Greece. Source Nino Arena.

▲ Officers of the *3rd Tank Battalion L* in Albania. Source: Ratti Archive.

▼ An L tank and some tank drivers at a halt during the advance towards Ioannina. Source: *In the Devil's Gardens* - D. Campini - Longanesi 1969.

▲ Three Italian tank drivers from *6th Company* of *III Tank Battalion L* during the maintenance of an L3/35 Tank. Source: Ratti Archive.

▼ An L3/35 tank destroyed by Greek fire in the Vojussa Valley. The employment of Italian armoured vehicles on the Greek-Albanian front was very unsuccessful. Source: *The Klisura Bridge. I carristi italiani in Albania 1940-1941* - R. Panetta - Mursia 1975.

▲ Infantrymen of the *3rd Tank Battalion L* in front of an L3/35. The soldier in the centre is still wearing a 1937 model jacket with a blue lapel - introduced in 1936 for the motorised and tank units - with the red two-pointed flames of the tank men. Source: Ratti Archive.

▼ Flame-throwing L-tanks of the *3rd Tank Battalion* in Albania in 1942. Note the inscription 'LF' [Flamethrower] on the flammable liquid tank.

▲ L3/33 tank of the *31st Carrista Infantry Regiment* in Albania. Source: Ratti Archive.

▲ Greek soldiers in the winter of 1940-41 with a 45 mm Brixia mortar captured from the Italians.

▼ Greek artillerymen with an 85 mm Schneider gun during the Italo-Greek war.

▲ The new M13/40 tanks also had little success during the campaign. In this case the tank of Second Lieutenant Galli of the 4th *Tank Battalion M* was destroyed by Greek artillery on 19 March 1941 on the slopes of Quota 731. Source: *The Klisura Bridge. I carristi italiani in Albania 1940-1941* - R. Panetta - Mursia 1975.

▼ Lieutenant Passalacqua's M13/40 tank hit by Greek artillery on 13 January 1941 near Klisura. Source: *The bridge of Klisura. I carristi italiani in Albania 1940-1941* - R. Panetta - Mursia 1975.

▲ Greek soldiers and officers pose with a newly captured M13/40 tank.

▼ Not only L3 tanks and M13/40 tanks were present in Albania. There were also a few old FIAT 3000s from the *1st* Frontier *Tank Company* - assigned to the Frontier Guard - which became part of the *3rd L Tank Battalion* from June 1942.

▲ L tanks, with their crews, waiting for Victor Emmanuel III's review in May 1941.

▼ Bersaglieri motorcyclists during the parade in Durres on 24 April 1939.

▲ Three Bersaglieri look at publicity posters for the film 'Big Shoes' at the Durres cinema in 1940.

▲ A large flag of the Kingdom of Italy hanging in a street in Tirana on 16 April 1939. Source: Niccolò Lucarelli - Italians in Albania 1939 1945 - Delta Editrice.

▼ Pavesi P4/100 artillery tractors during the Durres parade on 24 April 1939.

▲ Italian officers in front of a refreshment post for the wounded run by the Albanian Fascist Party during the conflict with Greece. Source ACS.

▼ Gunner and servant of the *15th Assault Black Shirts Legion 'Leonessa'* deployed in Albania in 1941. Source ACS.

▲ Goliardic photo of a group of Alpine soldiers of the *3rd Alpine Division 'Julia'* on the Greek-Albanian front. Source: Lombardy Cultural Heritage.

▼ A unit of the *6th 'Lancieri d'Aosta' Regiment* intent on crossing the Kalamas River in the early days of the war against Greece.

▲ Mules of an Italian tank division on the Greek-Albanian front. The absence of major roads and the mountainous terrain forced both Italians and Greeks to use these animals to supply their soldiers.

▼ Famous photo of a machine gunner and two infantrymen of the *49th Infantry Division 'Parma'* deployed in the Albanian mountains in the winter of 1940/41.

▲ Greek soldiers intent on carrying a heavy weapon.

▼ Bersaglieri and L tanks during a simulated propaganda attack.

▲ Italian officers and soldiers pose in front of a FIAT 626NLM [Nafta Lungo Militare] in Albania.

▼ Two financiers and a Carabiniere on guard at a post on the Greek-Albanian front. Source: ACS.

▲ Greek soldiers reusing some L tanks captured from the Italians. These vehicles merged into the 19th Motorised Division seeing rare use at the front..

▼ Truck of the *Reparto Munizioni e Viveri [R.M.V.]* of the *21st Reggimento d'Artiglieria 'Trieste'*, belonging to the *101st Motorized Division 'Trieste'*, sent to the Greek-Albanian front between 1940 and 1941. Source USSME.

▲ 81 mortar position of the *11th Infantry Division 'Brenner'* on an Albanian mountain in 1941. Source USSME.

THE LOSSES

Italian losses, according to Annex No. 6 of the *Report on Military Action in Albania on 7, 8 and 9 April* 1939 prepared by General Guzzoni in May 1939, amounted to:
- Officers: one killed and 18 wounded;
- NCOs: one killed and eight wounded;
- Troops: 10 killed and 64 wounded.

It is attested that most of the fallen were part of the *Regia Marina*.
In the book Albania at War 1939-1945, by Bernd Fischer, it is stated that the Italians suffered at least 700 losses, of which only 200 were in Durres.
Albanian casualties are unknown, Fischer estimates them to be higher than the Italian ones, thus above 700 men, but there are no certain figures.

CONSIDERATIONS ON ITALIAN OPERATIONS

There is no doubt that the operation was badly organised and had major problems, especially from a logistic point of view; the Chief of Staff of the Foreign Minister, Filippo Anfuso, himself declared to Ciano that '[...] if the Albanians had a well-equipped firing brigade, they could throw us back into the Adriatic [...]'.
However, the problems were also emphasised by the already mentioned Report *on Military Action in Albania on 7, 8 and 9 April 1939* written by General Guzzoni in May 1939 and the *Report on the Inspection carried out in Albania between 19 and 26 June 1939* written on 29 June 1939 by Chief of Staff General Pietro Badoglio.
In both, many problems are pointed out such as the large number of recalled soldiers who did not know how to use the new weapons or, even worse, a large number of Bersaglieri cyclists, especially of the 1901-1904 classes, who did not know how to use bicycles and motorbikes.
An even worse situation was that of the radio links, which had major problems caused mainly by the poor use of two-way radios by untrained soldiers.
This was caused by a lack of training at all levels and Badoglio himself stated in his report that it took a good two months of training to amalgamate the troops.
Guzzoni was also harshly criticised for the air-landing action of the two Grenadier battalions in Tirana, which was carried out so slowly that it took 2 hours and 55 minutes, from 10.05 a.m. to 1 p.m., for both battalions to disembark from the planes, with an average of 1 hour and 25 minutes per battalion.
Both described the terrible mistake of landing drums of fuel oil, instead of drums of petrol, in the port of Durrës on the night of 7 April, while Badoglio also had harsh words for the officers, half of whom were complements.

▲ Albanian Fascist Militia during a parade.

▼ Two soldiers in training with a FIAT-Revelli 1914/35 machine gun. The Albanian fascist militia saw wartime employment against Greece and in Kosovo. Source: *Albanian units in World War II* - Luigi Manes.

THE UNION OF ALBANIA WITH THE KINGDOM OF ITALY AND THE INCLUSION OF THE ALBANIAN ARMED FORCES IN THOSE OF ITALY

On 12 April 1939, the Provisional Administrative Committee, created on 7 April after the flight of King Zog, convened an Assembly that approved the union between the Kingdom of Albania and the Kingdom of Italy, appointing Shefqet Verlaci as Albanian Prime Minister, while on 16 April King Victor Emmanuel III was appointed King of Albania.
The Albanian armed forces were then merged with the Italian ones, while the advent of Albanian fascist institutions was completely new.

THE ALBANIAN FASCIST PARTY AND THE ALBANIAN FASCIST MILITIA

The fascistisation of the country began with the birth of the Albanian Fascist Party (in Albanian Partia Fashiste e Shqipërisë), while in September, the Albanian Fascist Militia was born, based on the Italian Milizia Volontaria per la Sicurezza Nazionale, divided into four Legions - the 1st based in Tirana, the 2nd in Corcia, the 3rd in Valona and the 4th in Shkodër - and 10 Cohorts.
Two special militias were also established, the Fascist Forest Militia, which had a Legion - 12th Legion - and the Albanian Road Militia (in Albanian Milicija Shqiptare e Rruges), created in January 1940.
In September 1940, the 1st Assault Black Shirts Legion 'Skanderbeg' was formed, which, with a platoon from the 2nd Battalion, took part in the first war action of the Greek campaign with the conquest of the Perati Bridge and the surrounding hills at 5.30 a.m. on 28 October 1940.
The 1st Legion, however, did not fight well and was withdrawn from the front as early as November 1940 and then finally disbanded on 30 May 1941.
From the middle of 1941, Albanian Black Shirt units were used to counter Albanian partisans as well as occupying parts of Kosovo, which had become part of Albania since 1941.
Here, Albanian Black Shirt units operated with extreme ferocity against the Serbian population of Kosovo, committing heinous crimes.

ALBANIAN UNITS OF THE ROYAL ARMY

The Albanian armed forces were united with the Italian armed forces on 13 July 1939 and from the autumn of the same year, Albanian infantry battalions and batteries assigned to the Italian infantry and artillery regiments were established.
By November 1939, there were six infantry battalions, which retained the names already

used in the Albanian army, with three rifle companies and an accompanying weapons company; the *23rd Infantry Division 'Ferrara'* was assigned the battalions *Gramos* and *Dajti*, the *7th Infantry Division 'Lupi di Toscana'* the *Korata* and *Kaptina* while the battalions *Tomori* and *Tarabosh* were attached to the *83rd Infantry Regiment 'Venezia'* and the *3rd Grenadier Regiment* respectively.

However, the staffing of these battalions was changed shortly afterwards to be identical to that of the Italian infantry battalions, consisting of three rifle companies and one machine-gun company, while the *Korata* and *Kaptina* battalions were transferred to the *53rd Infantry Division 'Arezzo'* and the *Tarabosh Battalion* to the *84th Infantry Regiment 'Venezia'*. The batteries, four in number, were all equipped with four 75/13 howitzers and retained the names of the Albanian batteries, being assigned to one Alpine artillery regiment - *Mathi Battery* - and three divisional artillery regiments - *Vijosa, Seman* and *Drin* Batteries.

In September 1939, six *Albanian Regional Volunteer Battalions were formed*, recruited in the south of the country; the battalions, commanded by an Albanian officer, were assigned to Italian divisions and their members did not wear uniforms but were provided with an armband and armed with Rifle 91.

Their constitution was a failure, however, as only 1,000 of the approximately 2,000 planned volunteers showed up and their staffs were very undersized, with some units not even reaching 100 men.

With the outbreak of World War II, the Albanian units saw their numbers increase thanks to the call to arms of several men through the establishment of five military districts - 131st Tirana, 132nd Shkodra, 134th Durres, 137th Berat and 139th Korcia - in May 1940.

With the entry of the Kingdom of Italy into the war in June 1940, 1,500 men of the class of 1917 were called to arms in July, with which the staffs of the six infantry battalions were completed and two counter-aircraft machine-gun battalions, each consisting of 4-5 companies, were formed for the defence of Albanian towns.

On 28 October 1940, the day of the Italian attack on Greece, the *23rd Infantry Division 'Ferrara'* was lined up with the *Gramos* and *Dajti* battalions, with about 800 men each, and the *Drin Battery*, while with the other divisions were the six *Regional Volunteer Battalions*.

The remaining infantry battalions were hastily sent to their assigned divisions.

The performance of these battalions, including the volunteer battalions, was very disappointing, with many desertions and units disbanded at the slightest Greek attack[27], so much so that they were already withdrawn from the front in early November.

The infantry battalions and batteries, with the exception of *Drin*, which had fought well, were gathered in Shijak and merged into the *Albanian Battalion Group 'Skanderbeg'*; some battalions were used to guard the border with Montenegro after the July 1941 uprising.

In the autumn of 1941, the *1st Albanian Infantry Regiment* was formed, consisting of the *Gramos* and *Korat* battalions and *Vijosa Battery*, followed in January 1942 by the *2nd - Tarabosh* and *Dajti* battalions *and Mathi Battery* - and the *3rd - Kaptina* and *Tomori* battalions *and Drin Battery* -.

---

27 After the withdrawal from the front, the *Dajti* and *Gramos* battalions *had a* strength of only 450 men each. Losses amounted to about 400 men per battalion, mostly deserters or prisoners. Taken from *Gli albanesi nelle forze armate italiane*, op. cit in bibliography.

These three regiments changed their names in March to the *'Hunters of Albania' Regiments*, which operated under Italian divisions with occupation duties.

In February 1943, the establishment of the *1st 'Albanian Hunters' Brigade'* was arranged, formed from the *1st Regiment* and the still non-existent *4th*; however, this never saw the light of day.

With the succession of defeats for the Axis forces, the situation with the Albanian forces got worse and worse and in May 1943 there were still 418 officers, 660 non-commissioned officers and 6,204 troop soldiers in the *Royal Army*, but the coup de grace came with the fall of fascism on 25 July, leading to an explosion of desertions[28].

On 4 August, the *2nd* and *3rd 'Albanian Hunters' Regiments* were disbanded and the rest of the Albanian units were affected by the Armistice on 8 September, disbanding; their members either passed into the ranks of the partisans or collaborated with the German forces.

GENDARMERIE AND ROYAL CARABINIERS

The *Gendarmerie* was incorporated into the *Royal Carabinieri Force*, part of the *Royal Army*, on 13 July and the following month, the *High Command of the Royal Carabinieri of Albania* was established, consisting of two *Legions* - Tirana and Vlora - with a total of 31 *Companies* and 42 *Lieutenancies*.

Most of the personnel were Albanians, who made up two-thirds of the Armed Forces in Albania; they immediately worked to fight criminals and recover weapons and ammunition.

With the entry into the war, the Carabinieri acted in various spheres, some units fought at the front assigned to Italian divisions and fought well, such as the *Mobile Carabinieri Battalion of Albania,* which defended Korcia, while other units operated against deserters and fugitives, with excellent results.

But not all that glitters is gold, and the scourge of desertion also affected the Albanian Carabinieri; from 1942, due to repeated partisan attacks on the barracks, the Italian forces were forced to abandon the outlying stations, which was viewed with suspicion by the Albanian Carabinieri, who began to desert.

In January 1942, the *Gendarmerie,* formed only by Albanians, was reconstituted, which gathered together all Albanian Carabinieri and gave a tough body to the *Royal Carabinieri*; in March 1943, the two Legions, by then formed only by Italians, were disbanded and the Carabinieri assigned only to military police duties, while all other duties were passed to the *Gendarmerie*.

With the occupation of Yugoslavia and Greece, some Albanian Carabinieri units operated in opposition to the local partisans.

BORDER GUARD AND ROYAL GUARD

The *Border Guard* was incorporated on 13 July 1939 into the *Regia Guardia di Finanza*, which in Albania was initially structured into 47 *Lieutenancies* and 143 *Brigades*.

---

28 Of the *2nd 'Albanian Hunters' Regiment,* 581 men deserted between 30 and 31 July and of the *3rd*, 400 men. Taken from *Gli albanesi nelle forze armate italiane,* op. cit in bibliography.

Again, most of the personnel were Albanians and with the outbreak of war, three battalions were formed, also thanks to the recall of 1,000 men of the 1916-17 class who had already served in the *Border Guard*.

At the beginning of the conflict with Greece, some units of financiers fought along the border and the Albanian elements initially fought well, but with the Italian reverses and the Greek penetration of Albanian territory, the climate changed.

Desertions began and in December the three battalions were disbanded, leaving only one battalion composed entirely of Italians, while two detachments were formed with the Albanians.

In 1942, the *Regia Guardia di Finanza was* re-staffed in Albania, being formed into two *Legions* that obviously had Albanian elements on their staff, which did not cause any major problems until the end of the year.

From the beginning of 1943, desertions increased dramatically, mainly caused by partisan attacks; at the Armistice, the remaining Albanian financiers went to the Germans.

ALBANIAN ROYAL GUARD

The *Albanian Royal Guard was* already included in the *Royal Army* as a battalion on 16 April and was transferred to Rome at the headquarters of the *2nd Grenadier Regiment* in the 'Principe di Piemonte' Barracks.

The members of the *Albanian Royal Guard were* sworn in on 29 April, and in May, Pariani opted for the establishment of an entire regiment, which was not done due to the lack of recruitable men given the strict recruitment rules that required volunteers or soldiers with at least six months' service and a height of at least 5'4".

The soldiers of the *Albanian Royal Guard wore the* gala uniform, which was made up of the traditional garments used in northern and southern Albania.

The unit remained in Rome until the Armistice, carrying out minor training and guarding the Quirinale until, left with just 118 men, it was disbanded.

▲ Albanian Black Shirts during a review. Source USSME.

▲ Two *Albanian Forest Militia* soldiers in gala uniform. Source USSME.

▼ Grenadiers of the *3rd Regiment* put the stars, symbol of the Italian soldier, on the Albanian soldiers of the *Tarabosh Battalion*. Source USSME.

▲ Albanian officers and soldiers of the Tarabosh Battalion ready to swear allegiance to the King of Italy on 23 July 1939. Source USSME.

▼ The Head of Government and Duce Benito Mussolini visiting the Albanian volunteers in March 1941 in Berat. Source USSME.

▲ A group of Albanian officers belonging to an *Albanian Hunters* Regiment. Note the variety of uniforms made up of both cord and grey-green cloth. Source: *Albanian units in World War II* - Luigi Manes.

▼ Two Albanian carabinieri, decorated with the Silver Medal for Military Valour, and the widow of another member of the Force who fell in combat against bandits and was decorated with the Gold Medal. Behind them an infantry officer is visible. Source USSME.

▲ Photograph of the swearing in of the *Albanian Royal Guard* in Rome on 29 April 1939. The Albanian soldiers swore allegiance by shouting Betoj! [I swear!] while the officers, individually, in front of the commander of the 2nd *Grenadier Regiment*. Source: *Albanian units in World War II* - Luigi Manes.

▼ Photograph of the handing over of the flag to the *Albanian Royal Guard*. Source: *Albanian units in World War II* - Luigi Manes.

ALBANIAN RESISTANCE UNTIL THE ARMISTICE

Immediately after the Italian occupation, the first acts of resistance began, but these were initially limited to the refusal to collaborate with the Italians, as mentioned by Ciano himself on 12 April 1939 when some secondary school students did not want to greet the Italians in a Roman manner or there were hymns to King Zog.

This hatred of the Italians was carried by both the nationalists - who had grown up with the myth of the War of Vlora - and the non-aligned population, who viewed the Italians badly, pointing at them as liars and, even though the Kingdom of Italy spent large sums of money in Albania, they believed that this money would be used exclusively for Italian interests.

Added to this was a bad Italian administration that only increased the hatred of the Albanians and even in 1940 there were some strikes by Albanian workers.

It was in 1940 that the first armed acts, often confused with simple armed attacks by Albanian brigands, began, and it was not until the summer of that year that there was the first 'big' revolt in Mirdita carried out by Catholic Albanians who feared that their sons would be conscripted and sent to the front.

From this period on, there began to be various attacks against Italian soldiers, especially in border areas, as in the case of a gang led by Ibrahim Kupi, brother of Abaz Kupi.

The turning point came after October 1940 with the serious Italian defeats against the Greek army, which shortly afterwards began to advance into Albanian territory, often receiving the support of the Albanian civilian population; on 17 May 1941, the 19-year-old Vasil Laçi made an attempt on the life of Victor Emmanuel III and Prime Minister Shefqet Verlaci but failed and was captured and hanged ten days later. Italian propaganda obviously tried to cover it up by claiming that the young man was of Greek origin.

In the meantime, the Albanian resistance, still unorganised, began to strike mainly at Italian links and lines of communication and at the end of 1941, the first real partisan bands were formed, which were organised by the *Communist Party* [*Partia Komuniste e Shqipërisë*], led by Enver Hoxha, who organised his forces into bands, consisting of between 50 and 60 men led by a commander and a political commissar, which obviously had the support of the Yugoslav Communist Party. In 1942, precisely on 16 September, following Comintern directives, Hoxha brought together in Peze the partisan commanders of all factions and the various local lords of the north and south of the country and founded the National Liberation Movement [*Lëvizja Nacional Çlirimtare*], which had the objective of uniting all Albanians in the struggle against the fascist occupier for the liberation of Albania.

Not everyone joined the MLN, and in November of the same year, some nationalist partisans and local lords founded the National Front [*Balli Kombëtar*], which became the counterpart of the communist forces in Albania.

The guerrilla actions increased and this led to the Italian reaction with the rounding up of as many as 27 Albanian districts throughout 1942 and the first major actions took place in the regions of Vlora and Peze but the clashes were few and the Italians, led by Marshal Logotito of the SIM, hit civilians - often using torture - and small towns in particular, leading to an increase in the number of men in the ranks of the Resistance.

The situation in 1943 could only worsen and the *9th Army* deployed in Albania had to clash frequently with partisan units, sometimes even getting the worst of it[1] since the Italian units were not trained in counter-guerrilla warfare and continued to use violence against the civilian population.

Partisan actions continued to strike Italian garrisons such as at Voskopoja, near Coriza, when 200 partisans succeeded in capturing 150 Italian soldiers and also took control of the town, while a few days later near Elbasan, 200 partisans, supported by 1,000 civilians, besieged several strongholds of the *41st Infantry Division 'Florence'*, capturing as many as 30 men.

In April 1943, the first Allied mission to the Albanian partisans arrived, sent by the Special Operations Executive, which parachuted in two agents: Lieutenant Colonel Neil Mclean and Major David Smiley.

The mission was aimed at organising airdrops to Albanian partisans and establishing contacts with Greek and Yugoslav formations but the first concrete results only came after the Armistice of 8 September.

In the meantime, the partisans continued to operate against the Italians, coming to control southern Albania; in March, 500 partisans attacked the fortified positions of the *49th Infantry Division 'Parma'* in Permet and were repulsed, while on 17 May, a strong partisan unit attacked the Italian garrison in Leskovik, defended by about 1,000 men. The attack was very hard and the Italians held out for three days until they were forced to retreat, leaving in the hands of the partisans a large booty of weapons and ammunition and losing hundreds of men dead and wounded and 30 prisoners in the battle.

In response, the Italians intensified their raids and in July carried out a harsh action between Mallakaster and Tepeleni - where they believed 2,000 partisans were deployed - razing some 80 villages to the ground and shooting hundreds of civilians.

By this time, however, much of the country was in the hands of the partisans and the sending of the *151st Infantry Division 'Perugia'* to Albania to replace the *'Ferrara'* sent to Montenegro was to no avail and on the eve of the Armistice, the *9th Army* deployed six infantry divisions in Albania.

The Armistice led the *9th Army* to dissolve and its units had different fates, almost all the divisions disappeared and their soldiers were interned by the Germans while the only division to resist beyond the Armistice was the *41st Infantry Division 'Firenze'* which clashed, together with elements of the *53rd Infantry Division 'Arezzo'*, with the Germans near Kruja on 22 September, being practically destroyed and forcing the survivors to flee to the mountains. From these men, who collaborated with the Albanian partisans, the *'Gramsci' Partisan Battalion was* born, which fought in the Resistance until the end of the war and even paraded in liberated Tirana on 29 November 1944.

---

[1] At the beginning of 1943, the garrison of the *49th Infantry Division 'Parma'* in Gjorm was attacked by 300 National Front partisans, being overwhelmed and losing 186 soldiers in combat. The subsequent Italian response was harsh and led to the killing of the Prefect of Vlora, who was considered a supporter of the partisans.

▲ Albanian partisans photographed in front of the Tirana road sign at the entrance to the city. Tirana was liberated by partisans in November 1944.

▲ Enver Hoxha, leader of the Albanian Communist Party.

▲ Lieutenant Colonel Neil Mclean, the first member of a British mission parachuted into the ranks of the Albanian Resistance.

▲ Italian partisans from the 'Gramsci' Battalion during the partisan parade in the city of Tirana on 29 November 1944. Source: Niccolò Lucarelli - Italians in Albania 1939-1945 - Delta Editrice.

▼ Albanian partisans during the parade in Tirana on 28 November 1944.

▲ *Balli Kombetar* partisans entered Prizren in 1944.

▼ Partisans of the *Balli Kombetar* posing; note the distinctly Italian armament.

▲ Italian gunner firing from a blockhouse in Montenegro. The situation was similar in Albania. Source ACS.

▼ A division of Blackshirts intent on carrying out a raid in Montenegro. Source ACS.

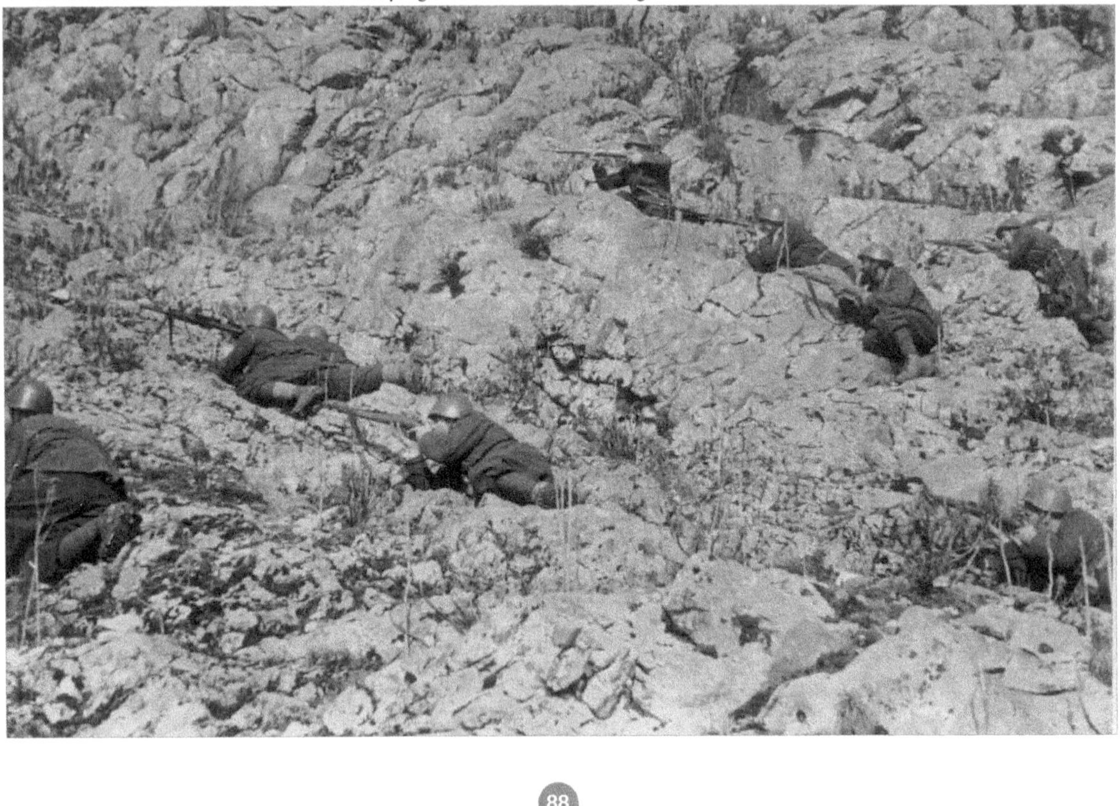

▲ The flags of the *'Gramsci' Battalion*.

▼ German defensive position in Albania near a river. Like all resistance forces, the Albanian partisans also tried to hit enemy lines of communication.

▲ Italian partisan squad in Albania. Source USSME.

▼ A large Albanian partisan formation moving towards Tirana.

▲ Posed photo of a group of partisans faking a fight in the city of Tirana.

▼ Vasil Laci after his capture following the assassination attempt.

▲ Albanian partisans posing. Note the many Italian weapons such as a Breda Model 1930 Machine Gun Rifle, two Beretta Automatic Muskets and a 91 Musket.

▼ Flag of the National Liberation Movement.

APPENDIX: ITALIAN DECORATORS DURING OPERATIONS IN ALBANIA

Of course, as in all military operations, there were soldiers decorated with Military Valour Medals.
As for the decorated, we list those awarded by Royal Decree of 22 September 1939-XVII and 9 August 1940-XVIII.

<u>Gold Medal for Military Valour</u>
- Lieutenant on Actual Permanent Service Riccardo Bombig of the *8th Bersaglieri Regiment*, decorated 'in memoriam' after falling in combat on the Drinassa Bridge 8 April.

<u>Silver Medal for Military Valour</u>
- Colonel Amerigo Anderson, commander of *Tactical Group 'Anderson'*, decorated for actions in Durres on 7 April;
- Colonel Tullio Bernardi, commander of the column of the same name, decorated for the good conduct of his department's actions;
- Private Damiano Blasi of the *47th Infantry Regiment 'Ferrara'*, decorated 'in memory' after being killed in Durres on 7 April while attempting to assault an Albanian position;
- Lance Corporal Achille Boccoli of the *3rd Bersaglieri Regiment*, decorated in memory after being mortally wounded in a clash with Gendarmes at Santi Quaranta on 7 April;
- Colonel Mario Carasi, commander of the column of the same name, decorated for his successful operations;
- Corporal Romolo Chirizzi, of the *47th Infantry Regiment 'Ferrara'*, decorated 'in memoriam' after being killed in a firefight in Durres on 7 April;
- Captain in S.P.E. Antonio Guarini, of the *91st Infantry Regiment 'Basilicata'*, decorated for his actions in Durazzo on 7 April;
- Bersagliere Domenico Landi, of the *9th Bersaglieri Regiment*, decorated in memory after being killed in a firefight between San Giovanni di Medua and Alessio;
- Bersagliere Iginio Milani, of the *9th Bersaglieri Regiment*, decorated because he was seriously wounded in a clash with Albanian troops in Alessio on 7 April;
- Lance Corporal Giovanni Moznich, of the *9th Bersaglieri Regiment*, decorated for continuing to incite his men, although seriously wounded, in a battle at Alessio on 7 April;
- Colonel Arturo Scattini, commander of the column of the same name, decorated for the good conduct of his troops;

- Bersagliere Pietro Sertori, of the *7th Bersaglieri Regiment*, decorated for being severely wounded while carrying out his duty as an order bearer;
- Second Lieutenant Bruno Zanetti, of the *8th Bersaglieri Regiment*, decorated for being wounded while attempting to recover the body of his commander during the clash at the Drinassa bridge on 8 April.

<u>**Bronze Medal for Military Valour**</u>
- Lieutenant Colonel Michele Adabbo, *8th Bersaglieri Regiment*, decorated for his actions in Durazzo on 7 and 8 April;
- Captain in S.P.E. Pietro Amodei, *7th Bersaglieri Regiment*, decorated for the capture of an enemy battery at Durazzo on 7 April;
- Carabinieri Captain Angelo Antico decorated for his actions in Alessio on 7 April;
- Corporal Gaetano Aricò, of the *10th Bersaglieri Regiment*, decorated for being seriously wounded at Bestrova on 7 April;
- Corporal Giuseppe Barresi, of the *10th Bersaglieri Regiment*, decorated for his actions in the battle at Bestrova on 7 April;
- Lance Corporal Elio Brigiotti, *7th Bersaglieri Regiment*, decorated for having conquered some enemy fire centres in Durazzo with his men on 7 April;
- Complement Captain Giovanni Chiaradia, of the *9th Bersaglieri Regiment*, decorated because on impulse, after taking the machine gun of a wounded bersagliere, he led his men to the conquest of a bridge near Alessio on 7 April;
- Staff Sergeant Antonio Cinco, from the *9th Bersaglieri Regiment*, decorated for actively supplying troops with his vehicle in Shkodra;
- Lieutenant Giovanni Covatta, of the *11th Bersaglieri Regiment*, decorated because he was wounded in Durazzo on April;
- Lieutenant Colonel Quirico D'Amico decorated for his actions as commander of the Engineer Corps in Shijak on 7 April;
- Major in S.P.E. Luigi De Micheli, assigned to command the Messe Column, decorated because he led soldiers in various actions in Durazzo to conquer enemy strongholds;
- Lance Corporal Antonio De Pascalis, of the *47th Infantry Regiment 'Ferrara'*, decorated because although wounded he continued to lead his men in the fighting at Durazzo;
- Aspiring Officer Lucani Fontani, of the *2nd Bersaglieri Regiment*, decorated because he led a platoon of motorcyclists towards Tirana, overcoming various enemy resistance;
- Captain in S.P.E. Antonio Gualano, of the *58th Infantry Regiment 'Abruzzi'*, decorated because he operated with a vanguard motorised column from Durres to Tirana;
- Major in S.P.E. Pasquale Lissoni, of the *'Anderson' Tactical Group*, decorated because he led several attacks against Albanian positions in Durres;
- Major Vincenzo Longo, of the *2nd Bersaglieri Regiment*, decorated because as the commander of a Bersaglieri battalion he performed brilliantly both in Durres and in the advance on Tirana;

- Lance Corporal Paolo Melcore, of the *47th Infantry Regiment 'Ferrara'*, decorated because although wounded he continued to lead his group during the fighting in Durazzo;
- Major in S.P.E. Mario Morra, of the *10th Bersaglieri Regiment*, decorated because he led his battalion during the fighting at Bestrova;
- Sergeant Major Vincenzo Panzella, of the *47th Infantry Regiment 'Ferrara'*, decorated because he continued to hold command of his squad even though wounded during the clashes at Durazzo;
- Lance Corporal Giovanni Pararusso, of the *9th Automobile Centre*, decorated because he hit an Albanian roadblock near Durrës with his vehicle and then participated in the conquest of the area;
- Second Lieutenant Mario Piccoli, of the *2nd Bersaglieri Regiment*, decorated because he and his platoon conquered an enemy position near Gusa on 7 April;
- Private Ernesto Portaluppi, of the *47th Infantry Regiment 'Ferrara'*, decorated for taking command after the death of his squad leader and then, leading his squad, conquered an enemy position in Durazzo;
- Sergeant Elio Pontoni, of the *11th Bersaglieri Regiment*, decorated because although wounded he continued to hold command of his squad leading to the capture of several enemy positions in Durazzo;
- Lieutenant in S.P.E. Ermanno Reatto, of the *2nd Bersaglieri Regiment*, decorated for his actions in Durazzo;
- Lieutenant Fermo Roggiani, of the *11th Bersaglieri Regiment*, decorated because although wounded he led his men to conquer several enemy strongholds in Durazzo;
- Bersagliere Carlo Robbioni, of the *7th Bersaglieri Regiment*, decorated because as a group leader he occupied several enemy strongholds in Durazzo;
- Lieutenant Colonel Ugo Scirocco, of the *9th Bersaglieri Regiment*, decorated for leading his men in the expansion of the San Giovanni di Medua bridgehead;
- Lance Corporal Antonio Stival, *8th Bersaglieri Regiment*, decorated for being seriously wounded in combat near Shkodra;
- Major in S.P.E. Pio Storti, of the *7th Bersaglieri Regiment*, decorated because as battalion commander he led his men to the conquest of Durazzo;
- Sergeant Achille Tomei, of the *11th Bersaglieri Regiment*, decorated because as the commander of a machine-gun platoon he led his men to the capture of a machine-gun post in Durazzo;
- Bersagliere Carlo Tonani, of the *3rd Bersaglieri Regiment*, decorated for having hunted down, together with others, a group of Albanian soldiers hiding in a house in Santi Quaranta;
- Major in S.P.E. Guido Turino, of the *11th Bersaglieri Regiment*, decorated because he led his men to the conquest of Durazzo;
- Bersagliere Sante Vendramin, of the *9th Bersaglieri Regiment*, decorated because although wounded he continued to fight in the clashes at Alessio;
- Captain in S.P.E. Michele Ventura, of the *9th Bersaglieri Regiment*, decorated because he led a company of Bersaglieri during the conquest of Alessio;

- Second Lieutenant Giacomo Visentin, of the *9th Bersaglieri Regiment*, decorated because as commander of a motorbike platoon he occupied several road junctions in the Alessio area;
- Colonel Giovanni d'Antoni, commander of the *Assault Tank Regiment of* the same name, decorated for his unit's action between Durres and Elbasan;
- Colonel in S.P.E. Alberto Mannerini, commander of the *Training Regiment of* the same name, decorated for his unit's airlift to Tirana airport;
- Lieutenant Colonel of Pilot Complement Fortunato Federici, of the *Messe Column*, decorated for leading some men to conquer enemy strongholds in Durazzo;
- Engineer Giovani Raina decorated for cooperating in disarming various enemy elements and securing a bridge in the Shyk and Sukthy area;
- Director of the *E.I.A.* concession Vittorino Romano decorated for his participation in the fighting in Durazzo and for collaborating in other actions;
- Engineer Raffaele Staccioli decorated for leading several units in Durres and towards Tirana.

There was also the awarding of 51 Croci al Merito di Guerra, which for reasons of space I will not list.

▲ Photograph of Lieutenant Riccardo Bombig, only Gold Medal for Military Valour during operations in Albania in April 1939.

BIBLIOGRAPHY

- Arena Nino, *La Regia Aeronautica 1939-1943. Volume Primo '1939-1940. Dalla non belligeranza all'intervento'*, Roma, Stato Maggiore Aeronautica Ufficio Storico, 1981.
- Battistelli Pier Paolo, *La guerra greco-italiana 1940-1941. L'errore fatale di Mussolini nei Balcani*, Gorizia, Leg Edizioni, 2022.
- Biagini Antonello e Frattolillo Fernando, *Diario Storico del Comando Supremo. Volume I (11.6.1940 - 31.8.1940). Tomo II (Allegati)*, Roma, Ufficio Storico Stato Maggiore Esercito, 1986.
- Crociani Pietro, *Gli albanesi nelle forze armate italiane*, Roma, USSME, 2001.
- Di Colloredo Mels Pierluigi Romeo, *Per vincere ci vogliono i leoni…I fronti dimenticati delle Camicie Nere 1939-1943*, Zanica, Soldiershop Publishing, 2019.
- Finazzer Enrico, *Guida alle artiglierie italiane nella Seconda guerra mondiale. Regio Esercito Italiano, Repubblica Sociale Italiana e Esercito Cobelligerante*, Genova, Italia Storica, 2020.
- Fischer Bernd Jurgen, *Albania at war, 1939-1945*, West Lafayette, Purdue University Press, 1999.
- Gallinari Vincenzo, *L'Esercito Italiano nel primo dopoguerra 1918-1920*, Roma, USSME, 1980.
- Longo Luigi, *L' Attività Degli Addetti Militari Italiani All'Estero Fra Le Due Guerre Mondiali (1919-1939)*, Roma, USSME, 1999.
- Lucarelli Niccolò, *Italiani in Albania 1939-1945*, Parma, Delta Editrice, 2021.
- Manes Luigi, *Le unità albanesi della Seconda Guerra Mondiale*, Zanica, Soldiershop Publishing, 2023.
- Montanari Mario, *Le truppe italiane in Albania (Anni 1914-20 e 1939)*, Roma, USSME, 1978.
- Pettibone Charles D., *The organization and order of battle of militaries in World War II. Volume IX. The overrun and neutral nations of Europe and Latin American Allies*, USA, Trafford on Demand Pub, 2014.
- Puletti Rodolfo e Dell'Uomo Franco, *L'esercito e i suoi corpi*, Roma. USSME, 1979.
- Ramoino Pier Paolo, *La Regia Marina tra le due guerra mondiali*, Livorno, Rivista Marittima, 2012.
- AA.VV, *Navi mercantili perdute*, Ufficio Storico dello SSM, Roma, 1997.

SITOGRAPHY

- www.angetmi.it
- http://www.niehorster.org/042_albania/Albania.htm
- https://naval-encyclopedia.com/ww2/minor-navies.php#al
- https://www.lavocedelmarinaio.com/2019/11/marina-reale-albanese-e-la-cannoniera-illiria/
- http://decoratialvalormilitare.istitutonastroazzurro.org/

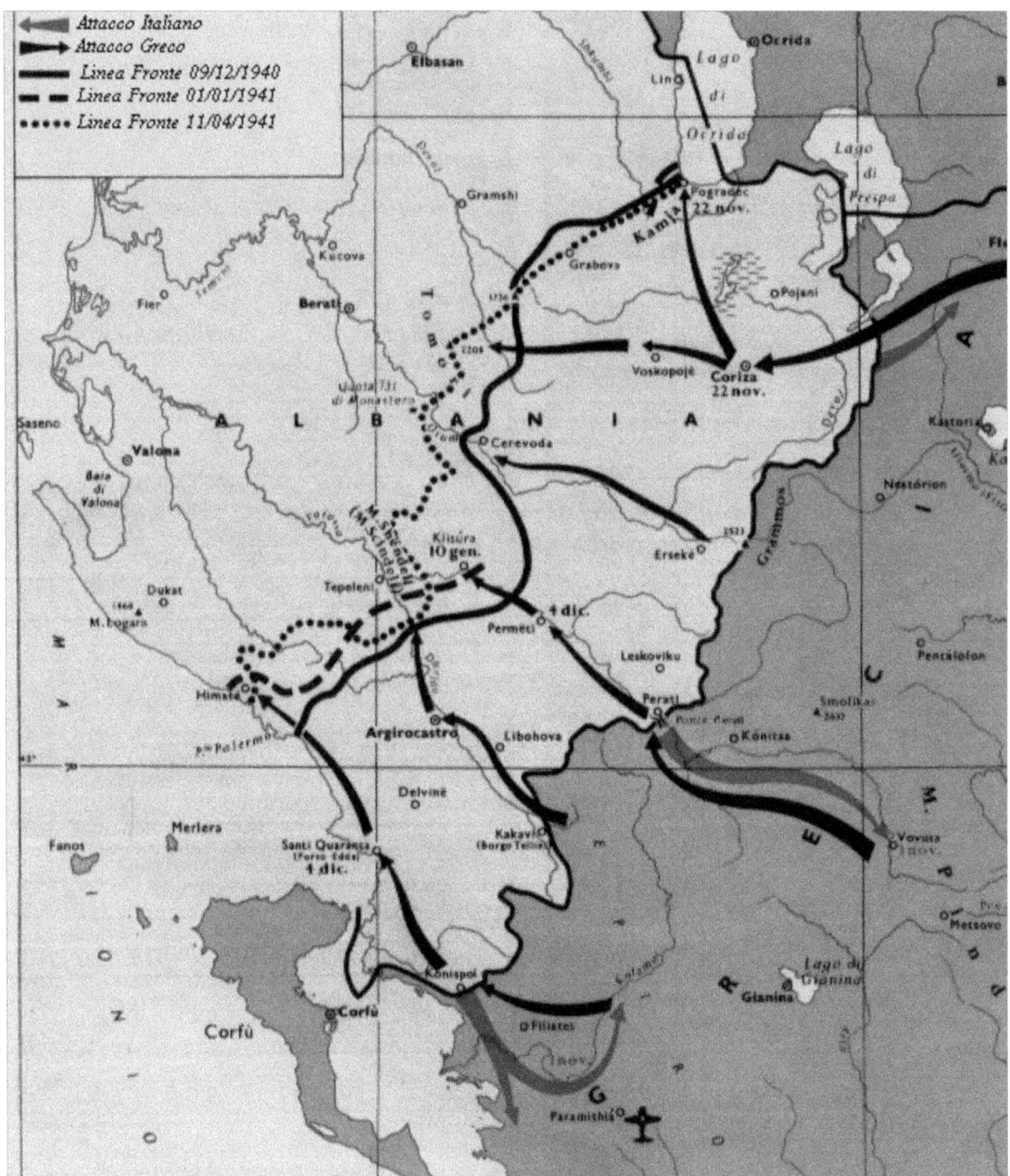

▲ Map of Greek penetration into Albanian territory. The Greeks conquered important settlements such as Santi Quaranta, Coriza and Gjirokastra.

TITOLI GIÀ PUBBLICATI - TITLES ALREADY PUBLISHING

BOOKS TO COLLECT

www.ingramcontent.com/pod-product-compliance
Lightning Source LLC
LaVergne TN
LVHW081451060526
838201LV00050BA/1768